Dreams Come True!

A little book on the power of words
By Jennifer Lynn Adams

Dreams Come True!
A little book on the power of words
By Jennifer Lynn Adams

ISBN-13: 978-0615882123
ISBN-10: 0615882129

First printing, September 2013
Flying Chickadee
PO Box 30021, Seattle, WA 98113-0021
www.flyingchickadee.com

All photographs, unless otherwise stated, are sourced from the Adams family collection
Photographs on Cover and pages 2, 8 by Laurie Gustafson ©2013
Photograph on page 14 by Jason Comerford ©2013
Photograph on page 20 by Heather Murray ©2013
Illustrations on pages 22, 24, 26, 28, 30 purchased and licensed for print use from istockphoto.com

For
Jeanne and James Adams

My Mother the Doctor and my Father the Author, who unconditionally support me in my journey towards success

What is your dream?

Hello, my name is Jennifer Lynn Adams.

Share your dream!

3

I was born with missing limbs.

Your dream can come true!

I grew up in a big family.

Good words and kind actions make dreams come true

I use a wheelchair to get from place to place.

All dreams are possible!

When I'm home I move around outside my wheelchair.

When I was a kid, other kids would tease
me because I looked different.

Everyone is special and every_one_has_a_dream

When kids teased me, it hurt my feelings
and made me scared to go to school.

I had a dream in my heart, that I would
be a singer when I grew up ...

My dream came true!

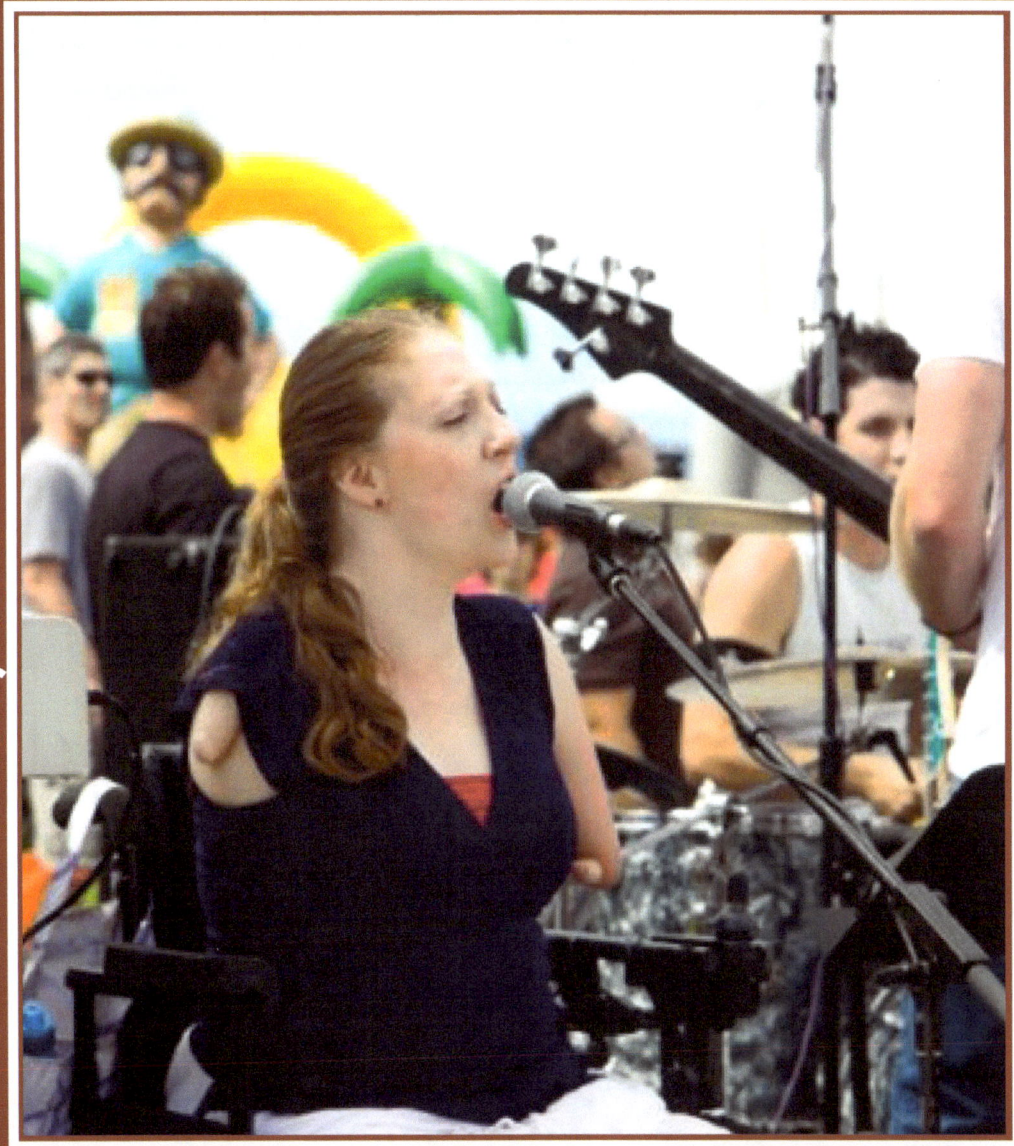

... so I stayed strong even when I was being teased.

When I grew up and went to college ...

kind words build others up

… I made friends who spoke true and
kind words to me.

A dream is something good you want to happen in the world

They said, "You are beautiful, your life
has purpose, your story will change lives."

Their kind words and friendship took
away the hurtful words from school…

Believe in someone else's dream

... and my dream of helping others with my words and talents came true!

Words have power!

Power to build up !

Or to tear down!

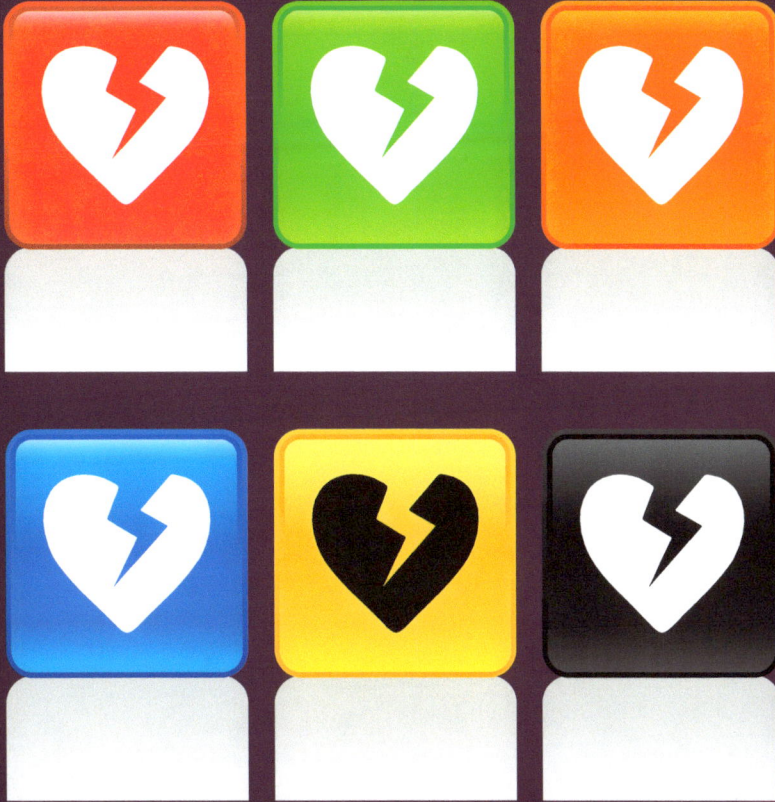

Your good words and kind actions are

powerful!

Start now.

Watch the power of your
good words and actions
build up others around you!

Say it out loud:

"My words have power!"

"I will use my words to build others up!"

"I will use my actions to help others around me!"

www.ingramcontent.com/pod-product-compliance
Lightning Source LLC
Chambersburg PA
CBHW041549040426
42447CB00002B/105